PUG
and OTHER ANIMAL POEMS

VALERIE WORTH

Pictures by
STEVE JENKINS

MARGARET FERGUSON BOOKS
Farrar Straus Giroux
New York

For Meg and Dan, Kate and Rob,
and Roxane and Conrad
—G.W.B.

For Jamie, Alec, and Page
—S.J.

FOX

Nearly a
Myth, his
Shady mask,
His flickering
Feet, his
Fiery tail;
Streaking the
Dark like
A fabulous
Comet—
Famous, but
Seldom seen.

MY CAT

Tamsine roams
The garden
Like an old
Familiar spirit,

Visiting the
Weedy fence,
Examining
The bushes,

Noting how
The wind revolves
And where the
Sun advances,

Printing every
Shimmer, every
Shadow, with
Her presence,

Which will
Stay to haunt
The place when
She is gone.

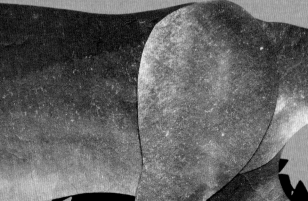

WOOD THRUSH

The blue jay cries
Away, away,
The cardinal calls
Come here!

But the wood thrush
Sings without words,
Filling the air with
Silver and water,

A brilliant language
Of leaves and rain
Too rare for
The human ear.

RABBITS

I like the
Way they ramble
Out of hiding

In the evening—
Daring
To be seen,

But staying
Far enough away
For safety—

And feed
Along the
Grassy fringe

Unhastily, in
Peaceful thought,
It seems.

BULL

When the earth
Shook forth
Great beasts
From its deep
Folds, gold
Fountains of
Lions, red lavas
Of horses flowing
Down, elephants
In soft gray
Pumice-tides,

The bull
Would not
Melt: but
Had to be
Hacked out,
Rough-hewn,
From the planet's
Hard side,
From the cold
Black rock
That abides.

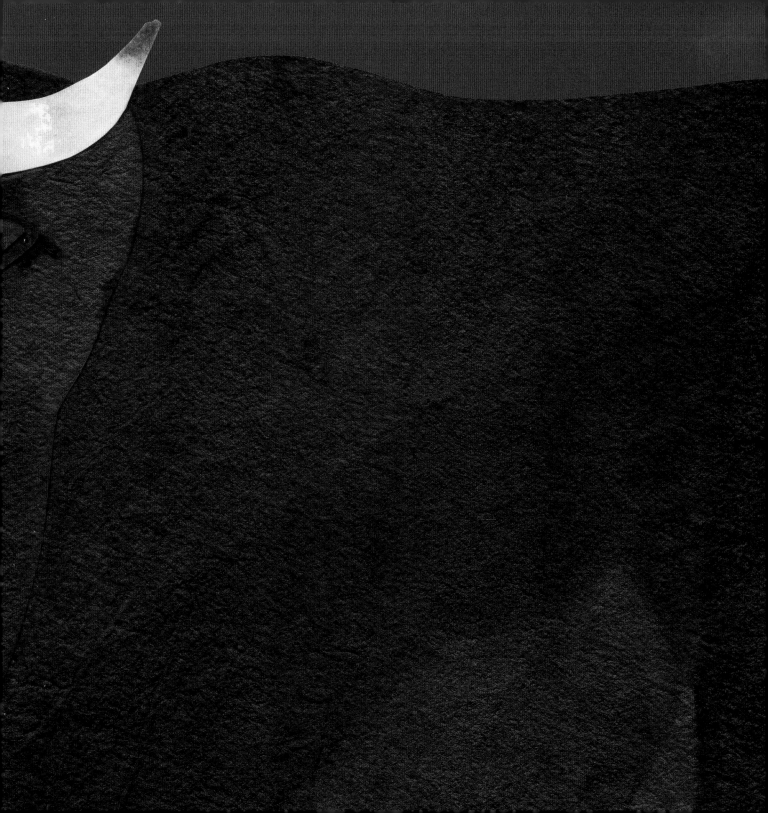

FISH

In these green aquarium
Windows, fish
Loom, rise and slide,
But all dulled
To the same white flesh,
Pale pictures, little more;
While where oceans
Rush unseen,
Fish flash in the shoals,
Clear-scaled, reflecting
Sun's gold, moon's pearl,
The silver-washed shore.

PUG

With their goggling
Eyes and stumpy
Noses, wrinkled
Brows and hairy
Moles, they're what
Some people
Might call plug-ugly;
Perhaps because, for
Dogs, they look
A lot like people.

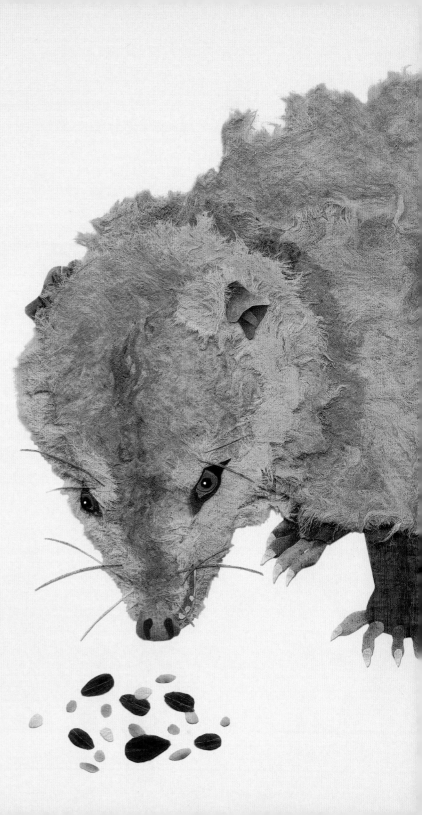

OPOSSUM

One year he appeared
In the yard,
Eating our birdseed
Spilled in the snow,

Chewing steadily, with
Teeth meant for meat,
Staring with serious
Eyes at nothing,

Busy, but slow,
As if thin fur, bare
Feet, the lean winter,
Were no matter.

GEESE

Then, they
Wavered away
Down the cold
Sky, with cries
Like grieving;

Now, we
Hear in those
Same high voices
Returning, a noisy
Rejoicing!

FLY

A fly stopped beside
One drop of sweet milk
We had spilled;
In a few minutes
He had drunk it all.
When he had finished
The spot was dry,
His gray belly filled
Quite round; then
Rising, rainbow-winged,
He was, slowly, gone.

BENGAL TIGER

The Bengal tiger
Batters his cage:
His rage is thunder,
Sharp stripes flash
In his fur—
Is it too wicked
To wish
He would break out,
Fill the zoo
With storms,
Run his lightning
Into the world?

FIREFLY

Tracked along the
Glitter of its
Slow constellation,
Scooped from the
Dark and caged
In the hollow
Of two hands,

It fills their
Cavern with
A cold pulse
Of enigmatic
Gold-green
Revelation, before
Slipping out

Between crossed
Thumbs, and slyly
Winking away,
Leaving the skin
Tinged with an
Alien astringent
Insect-smell.

TOADS

That house
Had shallow
Wells around the
Cellar windows,

Places all
Their own,
Holding a clutter
Of leaves,

Lost tennis
Balls and
Marbles, and
Sometimes

Leathery
Lumps of
Earth with
Gilded eyes.

MOUSE

Papery ears
Silk fur
Slim paws

Caught by
The cat
At midnight:

Left as a
Gift on
The step.

CICADA

A fairy
Tale come
True: the

Humped brown
Gnome split
Up the back,

The silver-
Caped prince
Set free.

DACHSHUND

It's hard
To keep
From drooping

When you've
Got so long
A body—

Plenty of
Legs at
Front and back

But nothing
Propping up
The middle.

SPARROWS AND PIGEONS

Even in winter, along
Streets of stone
Where a thin sun
Warms nothing,
Sparrows and pigeons
Seem at home,
Where there appears
To be no home,
Fed, where no hand
Feeds them: flying,
Alive, on roofs,
On ledges of windows,
Down in the alleys,
They seem at home
And warm—as if
It were the country
And summer here,
Summer always,
And high gold corn.

RAT

Any ruin
His bower,
His pleasure,

Any trash his
Treasure, the
Worse the better;

Out of our
Litter he
Builds a throne,

King in his
Castle of old
Rag and bone.

Farrar Straus Giroux Books for Young Readers
175 Fifth Avenue, New York 10010

Text copyright © 2013 by George W. Bahlke
Pictures copyright © 2013 by Steve Jenkins
All rights reserved
Color separations by Embassy Graphics Ltd.
Printed in China by South China Printing Co. Ltd.,
Dongguan City, Guangdong Province
Designed by Roberta Pressel
First edition, 2013
3 5 7 9 10 8 6 4 2

mackids.com

Library of Congress Cataloging-in-Publication Data
Worth, Valerie.
    Pug and other animal poems / Valerie Worth ; pictures by Steve Jenkins. — 1st ed.
        p.   cm.
    ISBN 978-0-374-35024-6
    1. Animals—Juvenile poetry.   2. Children's poetry, American.   I. Jenkins, Steve,
1952–   ill.   II. Title.

PS3573.O697P84 2012
811'.54—dc22

                                                                                    2010034300